CAN YOU HEAR ME?

A collection of poetry

By

YAMI GRAY

Kids4Kids

Can You Hear Me?
A collection of poetry

Published in the United Kingdom by Kids4Kids, an imprint of Pen & Ink Designs Publishing

Paperback edition ISBN: 9781912472550

Ebook edition ISBN: 9781912472574

First Edition: May, 2018

Category: Poetry

KIDS4KIDS.ORG.UK

The aim of the Kids4Kids Organisation is to promote children's books, most importantly those written by children. Formed in 2002 to work with the charity The John Hardy Trust, the Kids4Kids organisation was created to support young people. Initially, this was done through sport and by working alongside sporting goods suppliers.

Moving on, Kids4Kids now works alongside Mentoring Writers, an organisation that works with writers of all ages worldwide by helping them develop their writing skills.

By giving young people the opportunity to express themselves through the written word it allows them to grow and develop into well-rounded young adults.

If you are young person who wants to try writing a story then contact Kids4Kids.

Web: www.kids4kids.org.uk
Email: admin@kids4kids.org.uk

For the older writers check out the Mentoring Writers website:

Web: www.mentoringwriters.co.uk
Email: contact@mentoringwriters.co.uk

CONTENTS

Danger

Staring at myself
Reflection changes
Who am I?
Who are you?
My feelings are nothing but a toy
My mind is in danger
A fluid gender.
Mixing, matching, changing Once a girl, once a boy!

Alice in Wonderland

Lock me up, don't let me out
I'm losing myself in Wonderland.
I keep forgetting what reality is about
The curiosity is scaring me.
Searching, seeking
For what, I do not know
A queen, a cat
And a glimpse of a white rabbit.
Drink me, wine, medicine.
Eat me; food, pills.
Am I big, am I small?
Should I cry and ignore it all?
Down the rabbit hole and back
Tea with a hatter, hare and mouse
With nostalgic memories of the past.
Although I'm now trapped within a madhouse.
Cheshire, do not look for me.
Hatter, don't you know.
Running from the Bandersnatch
I'm Alice, in wonderland, watch…

Swallowing

Feelings changing
Heads shaking
Hands grabbing
Hearts aching
Gender hollowed
Tears wallowed
Bandages wrapping
Pills swallowed

Wanting

I lose the ones I love
No matter how hard I try
Play with fire and get burned
Not one single lesson I have learned

Wanting what I never had
Needing what is gone
The burning that is in my mind
Where is the peace that I can't find?

Can You Hear Me?

Alice, can you hear me? You're about to drown. Crazy non-stop laughter, While the Cheshire steals the crown.

Reality and dreams mixing they collide, with no sleep-in wait a one-off massive joy ride. Peaceful insanity better hold on tight, down the black rabbit hole screaming in fright.

She says 'dance 'til you die in this crazy dream that's gone.' Off with their heads one by wretched one. Twisting and turning breaking every bone. Growing and shrinking, to see if you'll atone. Alice, can you hear me?

You're about to drown.

Crazy non-stop laughter

While the Cheshire steals the crown.

So, Alice?

Can you hear me?

Darkness

Alone in an empty house

Whispering words echoing

Torment, torture, save me, save me

Tear me down and kill me

Insanity catching much like a flame

Damnation rising, feeling like dying

Pain and sorrow, written words

Full books, with marks of teardrops and blood

It's spreading, spreading

Changing, bending

Grotesque shapes of shadows passing

Alone, alone, alone tonight

Demons waiting, darkness reigning

Candle wax burning delicate hands

Windows shaking from wind and rain Blood pooling, pooling
and pouring

No-One

Keys leading to no-where
Empty bottles on the floor
Phones ringing endlessly
With no-one to answer the call
Bags broken and ripped
Laptop tight shining dull
Cards, thrown carelessly
And a mirror in the hall

Dedication to Great-Grandad Roy 1918-2011

The tears have fallen
Like rivers of Grief
Silent but hurting
And gone is another life.
Tears of sorrow corrupt me
They sing of fragile skin
But they are let be
And it starts all over again.
There are tears of pain
And it shall haunt my memories
But I am still living
At least.
Tearful days sweep on
But none without thoughts
Missing you ever more
For time and eternity.
As tears dry on sad faces
And the world rushes by
Resting in peace
Roy Greenwood

Seeing

See me, hear me
Am I different, can I change
Look at me, listen to me
I'm shouting, shouting out in vain

See me, hear me
Can I, will I, cry
Look at me, listen to me Screaming - why, why, why

See me, hear me
I can feel the suffocation Look at me, listen to me Wrapping
around, self-mutilation.

Memories

Paint a picture of happy memories
Rushing back to that place
Needing that same love
Yet, not knowing the difference
Is it true, is it false?
Are we only fake dreams?
So, I'll ask once more in this small voice of mine
Are we real; as I hope?
So real and divine
In a voice like a whisper, calling out your name
Are we done as I fear
Will I fall in such disgrace?
So, I will say goodbye and hope someday
That we'll both look back on these memories, we made.

Depths of the Night

Back into the depths of night
Bruised and torn I blunder
The demons laughing with delight
As in the darkness, I stumble

Roaming far and roaming wide
Wherever I may be
Always travelling in the dark
No one, only me

In the darkness, a cliff is found.
Below the cold crisp sea
Fast and hard I'm falling down
But in the sky, I wish to be

So back into the depths of night
Torn and cold I stumble
The demons giggle with no slight
As in the blackness, I blunder.

Standing Tall

Because I'm me doesn't mean you have to be a bitch
Because I'm different doesn't mean you have to hate it
Because I don't give a damn doesn't mean you have to like it

So, we are different and we honestly don't give...
We'd rather die in a hole than be like you

You can hate us and make us feel so low
But we will be standing tall
You can annoy the hell out of us
But we'll be standing ever more.
You can use all your ammunition
And all your bullets
But we won't shed a single drop

I had a life, baby we made a rainbow
I'm Missing; how you Miss me
Let's tell the world what we see

People, faces, different spaces
The time slowly slipping away
So, what do you say?

You can hate us and make us feel so low
But we will be standing tall
You can annoy the hell out of us But we'll be standing ever
more.
You can use all your ammunition
And all your bullets
But we won't shed a single drop
We don't need you
We're better off without you
So, go, go, go, go, go,
We don't need you
We're better off without you
So, go, go, go home and cry yourself to sleep...

You can hate us and make us feel so low
But we will be standing tall
You can annoy the hell out of us But we'll be standing ever
more.
You can use all your ammunition
And all your bullets
But we won't shed a single drop
But we won't shed a single drop

OH
And remember Karma is a bitch
See you, when I'm your boss...

Let Me Fly

I have wings But I cannot fly I am trapped in this cage, As the
days go by One day I'll be here again Starting over anew
Going to come back here once more And live, like I have
always wanted too Moving from place to place Year after
year
Never stopping or slowing my pace As my nightmares
disappear To dance across the moonlit sky It has always been
my dream But first I must learn how to fly And falling is my
fear Falling fast or falling hard Whichever may appear
The wind brushing past my mind Is all that I can hear
So goodbye cage that holds me fast This day I will escape
I do not expect this freedom too last But at least just for today

Passion, Soul and Nature

And here I am

At the end of my happiness

My tormented mind, so dark and dead For I search in silence.

As I write my soul on pages Remembering pain from

different ages My art shall be remembered Long after I die.

So, when I draw or when I write

The darkness, from my world, takes flight All the dancing

shadows, gone And disappears with all my wrong.

For art is my nature

Music my soul

Writing my passion 'Til I grow old...

Sorrow, Pain and Misery

Silently I cry
Obsessed with all the pain
Remembering the past
Recalling it in vain
Open to the hurt
While anger burns inside

Goodbye for now, or see you soon
Never again, Excluding you

Perpetually alone
A kind of sudden death
I had once known
Now nothing is left
But where are you now
When desire is in my heart

Goodbye for now, or see you soon
Never again, Excluding you
Memories of life
Ignorant or alone?
Sadness pays its price
Experience proved me wrong
Running from my heart
You chased me

Goodbye for now, or see you soon
Never again, Excluding you

Red Riding Hood

Perhaps it did not start with night
It could have been the horrors of humanity
The echoes of the steel axe
But I am just a wolf and you are my red cloaked riding hood.

Perhaps the stories tell my tale differently
After all, I am nought but an animal
And in this dirtied reality of yours
Am I really the dark wolf you have been warned against
When my fur becomes yours for hanging.

I often wonder why I am called a beast when I hunt only for
survival but your ilk and all their poisons Destroy the lands
around you.

Perhaps I did not howl for hunger but for the ache of
loneliness that grips me My cries sound through the dark
nights The moon being the companion I am guided by.

I am not evil, I am not cruel
I am merely alone and in need of company Surely a
connection is possible with you We are not completely
different are we.

Perhaps it did not start with night
I can remember your role quite clearly
and you're the girl in the cloak stained with my lifeblood My
little Red Riding Hood.

Reflections

Mirror reflections can lie
When I see me, I can only hate?
The way I look, my hair, my face
It gets confusing, am I a girl, am I a guy?
Shifting, changing, never ending
Each day a different feeling Who am I, what am I?

Binding tighter, tighter and tighter
Struggling, not breathing
Anything for change
Secrets supporting anger
Deep inside, sorrow lingers
I want to be a girl, I want to be a guy.

A fluid change, with a morning of horror Gender musing,
wondering, not belonging Can I hide, can I cry, can I lock
myself up inside Hate, fear, oppression
Happiness, love, acceptance
I can't change, I want to, I want to.

Say Goodbye

It's hard to say goodbye
When you're the only one
Chasing that dream
While the world turns to ash

Remember a time
A place to meet
Wanting what is no longer ours
I will keep fighting

For your ever-cold lips
Hoping, needing once more
Say goodbye and wish me to die
Roses for a dying love

A wish to keep fighting
For what we had
This never-ending parade
It's time for our feelings to fade

To leave with smiles on our faces
As we say our painful goodbyes

Snow White

It begins with expectation You're a girl, you must be pretty
Mother would tell you – 'You need more femininity'

Is it your skin that you need to hide Is it your body?
What's wrong with your size?

Look at the pictures
Miracle surgeries, impossible cures Looks are just temporary
but we can freeze yours?

Cut yourself up Swallow the poison Don't wake at all Your
prince is not coming.

Sleep around with a few men and clean up your messes.
No one likes a virgin we just need your confessions

So, doll yourself up, slim yourself down With red lips and a
pale face Mirror, mirror, Snow White is here.

Worthless

Unable to do anything, Me and myself
Imprisoned in darkness, Deep black
Like the blood in me
I don't know, Why won't I die

Seeping, inside my head
My own personal hell, Lonely and dark
Locked in a room, Void and unwelcoming
I know nothing at all, Of the warmth of another
I don't know, Why won't I die

My only companion, The insanity, the madness
Whispering sweet nothings
Twisting my reality
How do I do this?
I don't know, Why won't I die

I don't know how to deal with this

NB A poem inspired by the character of Crona from Soul Eater

Shadows of War

I am hunted by the shadows of war
The chaos of malicious conflict
Covering the earth with bodies
And innocent blood drips from my hands.

The fierce battle rages on
With many falling at my hand
Collapsing on the battlefield of despair
And death haunts my memories.

Fate has chosen this horrible destruction
Thrusting death upon those who fight
A thief for blood helping the chaos around me
For this is the heartless, merciless anguish that is war.

This book was published by:

Pen & Ink Designs Publishing

Cardiff, UK

Kids4Kids is an imprint of Pen & ink Designs
Publishing and is owned by Ann Brady

www.penandinkdesigns.co.uk

www.ingramcontent.com/pod-product-compliance
Lightning Source LLC
Chambersburg PA
CBHW021921040426
42448CB00007B/860